INTO THE VOLCANO

A GRAPHIC NOVEL
BY CALDECOTT HONOR ARTIST

Don Wood

THE BLUE SKY PRESS
An Imprint of Scholastic Inc. • New York

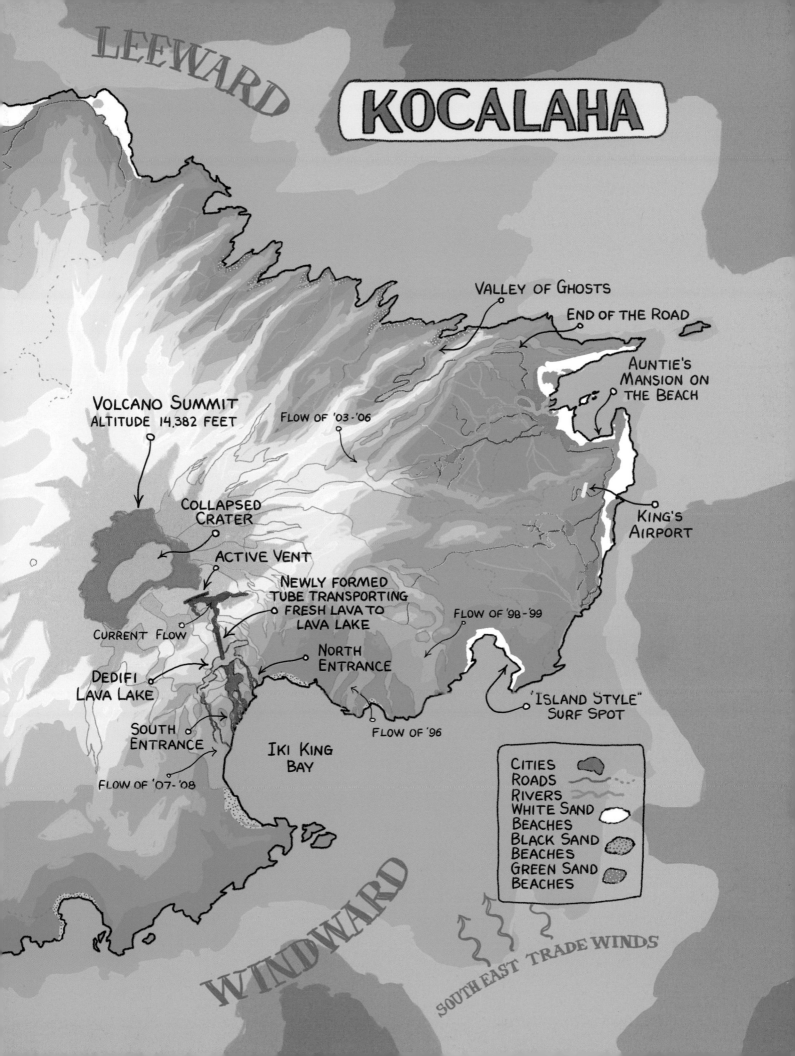

6

SUMO! WAKE UP!

GENTLEMEN, I AM CALLED AWAY ON URGENT BUSINESS. MY DRIVER WILL DELIVER YOU TO YOUR PLANE.

HERE... LET ME HELP YOU. I'M YOUR HOSTESS. YOU MUST BE FAMISHED. I'LL HAVE YOUR DINNER READY AS SOON AS WE'RE AIRBORNE.

STEAK, CHILI-FRIES, AND CHOCOLATE CAKE A LA MODE. IS THAT RIGHT?

WHERE ARE THE OTHER PASSENGERS?

11

20

WE ARE RUSHED. I CAN HEAR THE SURF BOOMING. LAVA IS FLOWING FAST.... THIS MAY NOT BE A GOOD IDEA...

...TOO DANGEROUS.

MY SON, YOU OF ALL PEOPLE!

YOU GET OUT THERE AND LEAD OUR FAMILY! DO WHAT MUST BE DONE!

✳@彡✳◗#彡彡! UPHOLD OUR HONOR!

IF THEY GET IT OFF THE ISLAND, IT'S GONE FOREVER.

OK. HEE-YAAAHH! LET'S GO!

WE CAN'T. TIDE'S WRONG. SURF'S UP. IT'S ALL WORSE THAN I THOUGHT. THAT HOT LAVA WILL COME DOWN AND TRAP US.

THE FLOW OF '96, '99, THE FOUNTAIN OF '07... NOBODY KNOWS LAVA IN THE WATER LIKE ME.

TAKE US IN.

I'LL GO IN AND NOSE AROUND, BUT NO PROMISES.

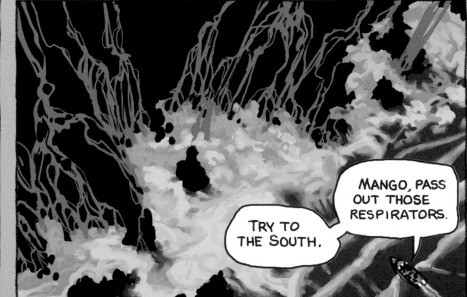

TRY TO THE SOUTH.

MANGO, PASS OUT THOSE RESPIRATORS.

I CAN'T BREATHE IN THIS THING.

PUT IT ON, AND KEEP IT ON, FOOL. THERE ARE GLASS PARTICLES IN THE SMOKE. IT WILL KILL YOU.

WITHOUT A RESPIRATOR, YOU'RE DEAD.

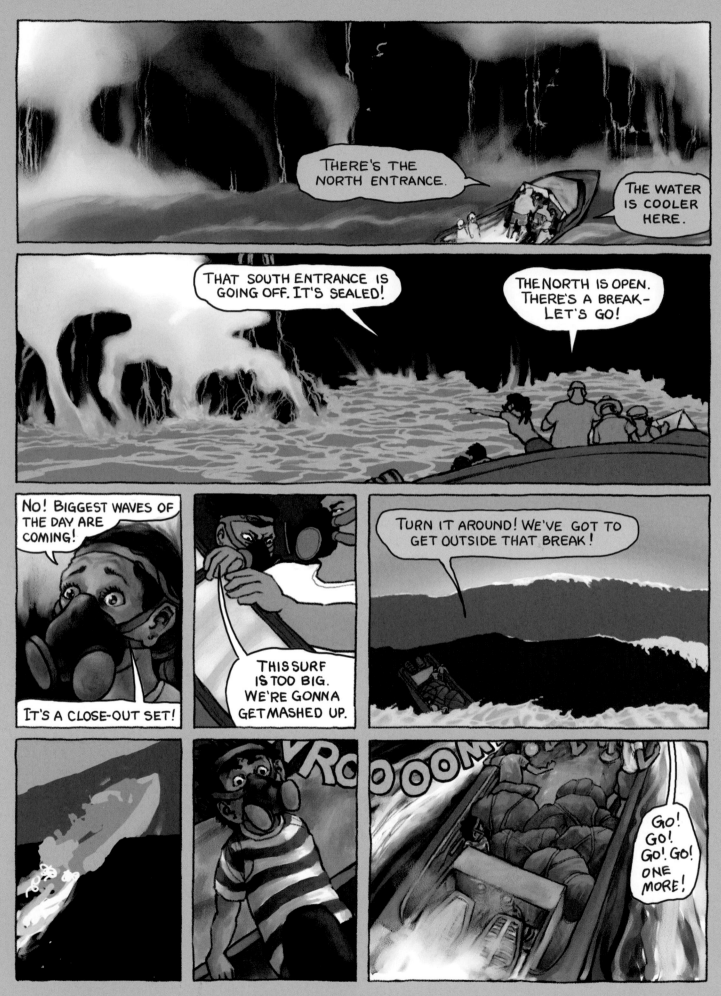

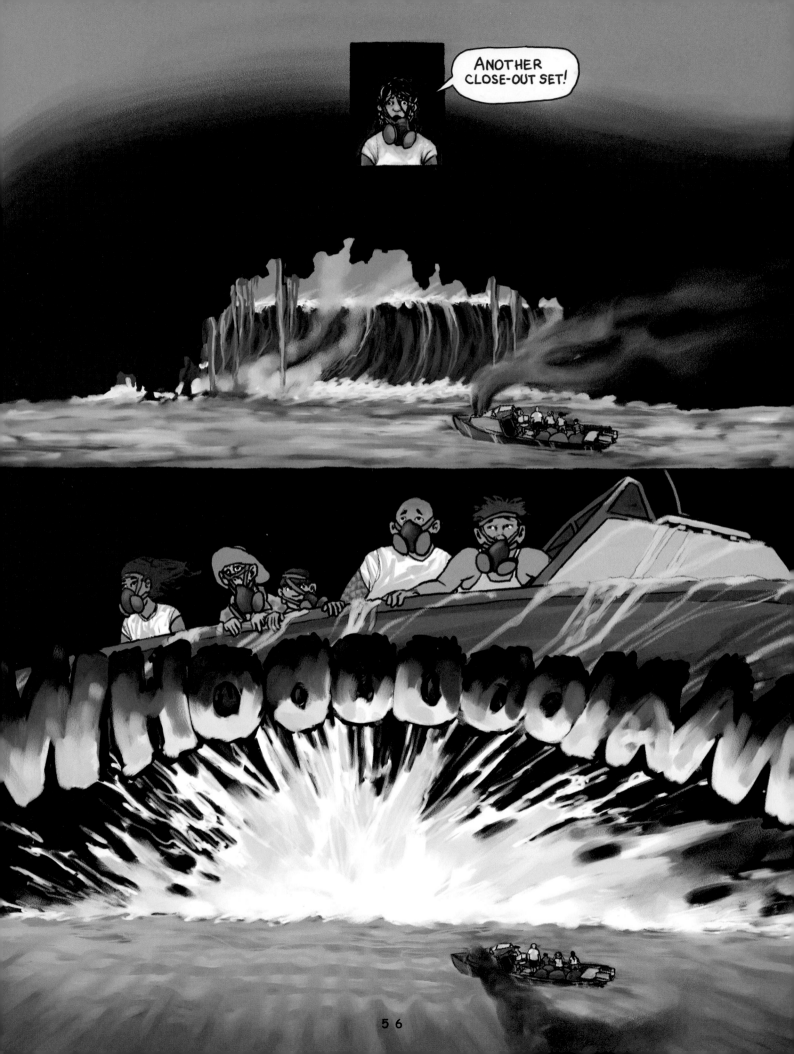

81

DUFFY! WHERE ARE WE GOING?

C'MON! C'MON!

LOOK!

YOU'VE FOUND YOUR AUNTIE'S CABIN.

SHE STAYED DOWN HERE BEFORE HER HEALTH DETERIORATED. AS YOU CAN SEE FROM ALL THE PHOTOS, SHE IS DEVOTED TO YOUR SIDE OF THE FAMILY.

WHERE'S MY MOTHER?

NOW YOU BOYS RUN ALONG....

GO ON BACK TO WHERE YOU'RE SUPPOSED TO BE, AND LET ME CONTINUE MY SEARCH.

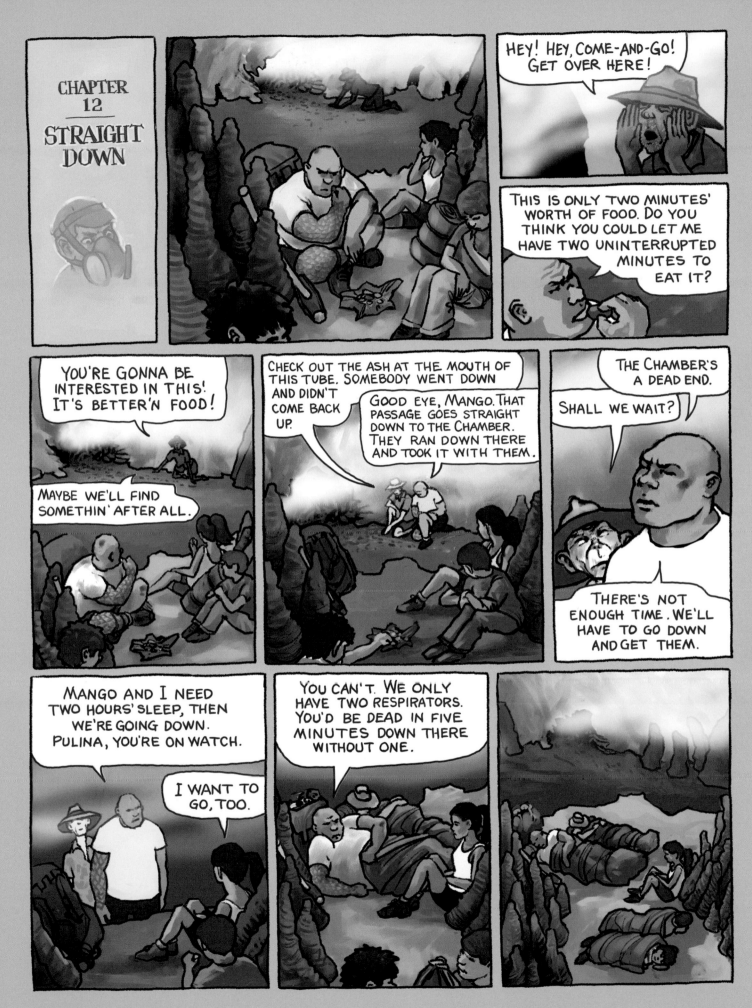

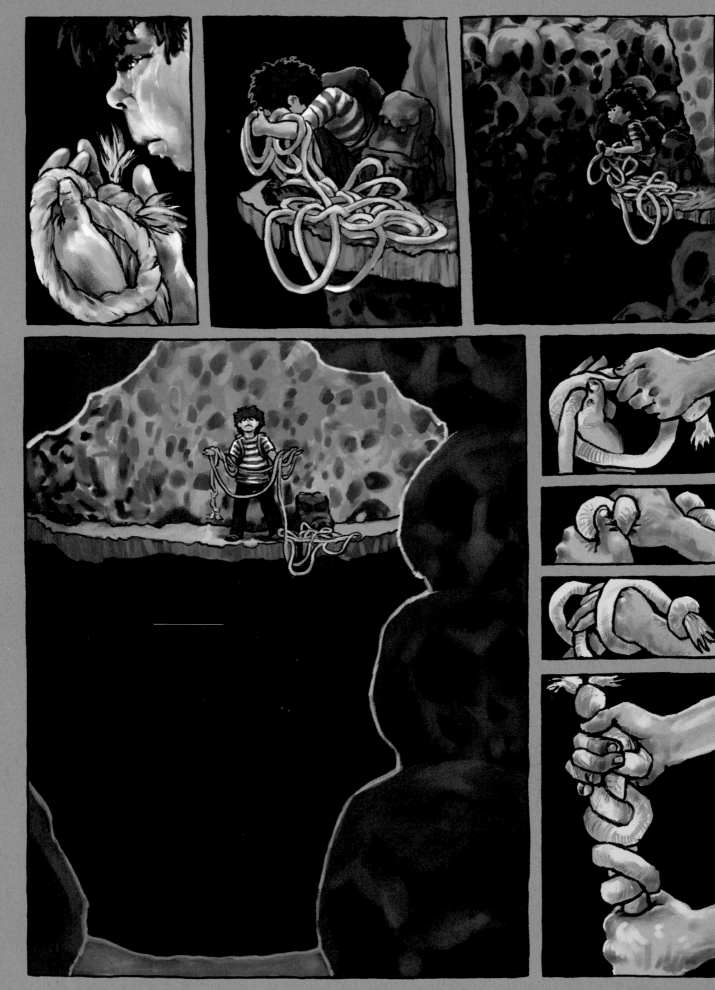

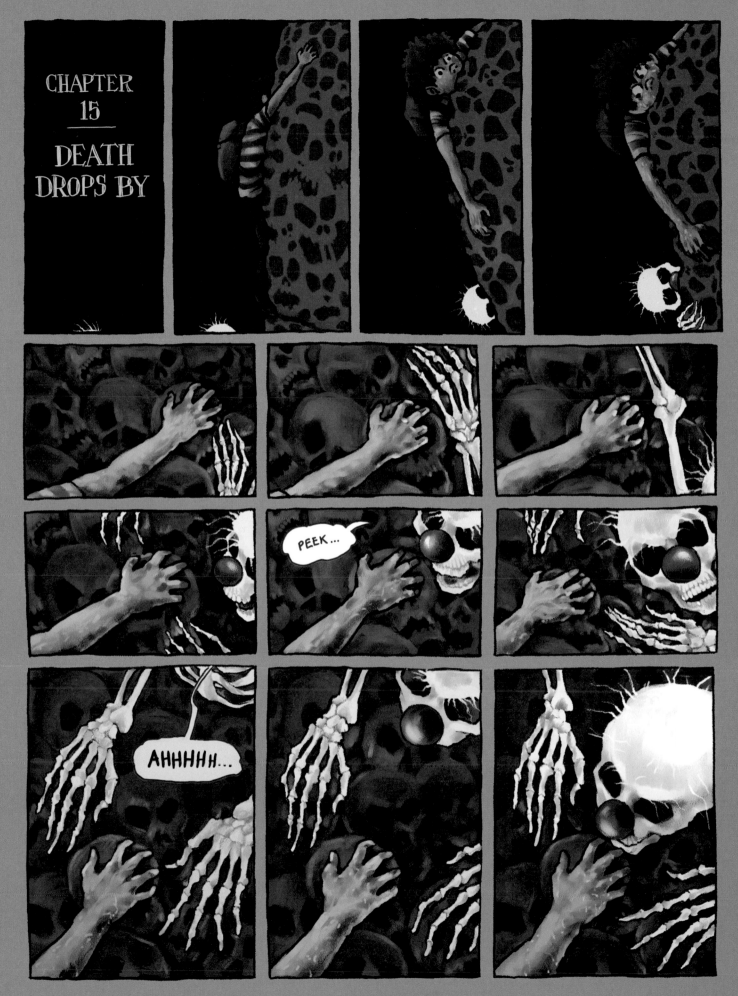

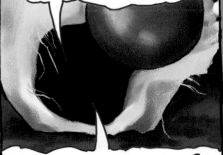

OR MAYBE...HEE-HEEEEEEEE... IT'S THE "FAILURE TO LIVE UP TO YOUR POTENTIAL" THING. YOU COULD HAVE BEEN A GREAT WHATEVER AND CHANGED THE WORLD.

HAW HAW HEE-HEEEEEEE....IF I HAD A NICKEL FOR EVERY TIME I'VE HEARD THAT ONE....

Y'KNOW...

IF YOU HAD FALLEN INTO THIS HOLE...

DUFFY WOULD HAVE RESCUED YOU.

WELL...I SEE THAT YOUR RIGHT LEG IS BEGINNING TO SHAKE....IT WON'T BE LONG NOW....

SO NOW THAT YOU'VE HAD YOUR LITTLE GESTURE OF DEFIANCE... I'LL JUST SLIDE ON DOWN INTO THE DARK PIT AND WAIT FOR YOU....

♪♫ DUM-DEE-DOO-DEE-DOO... ♫

DOODLE-DEE DAH...

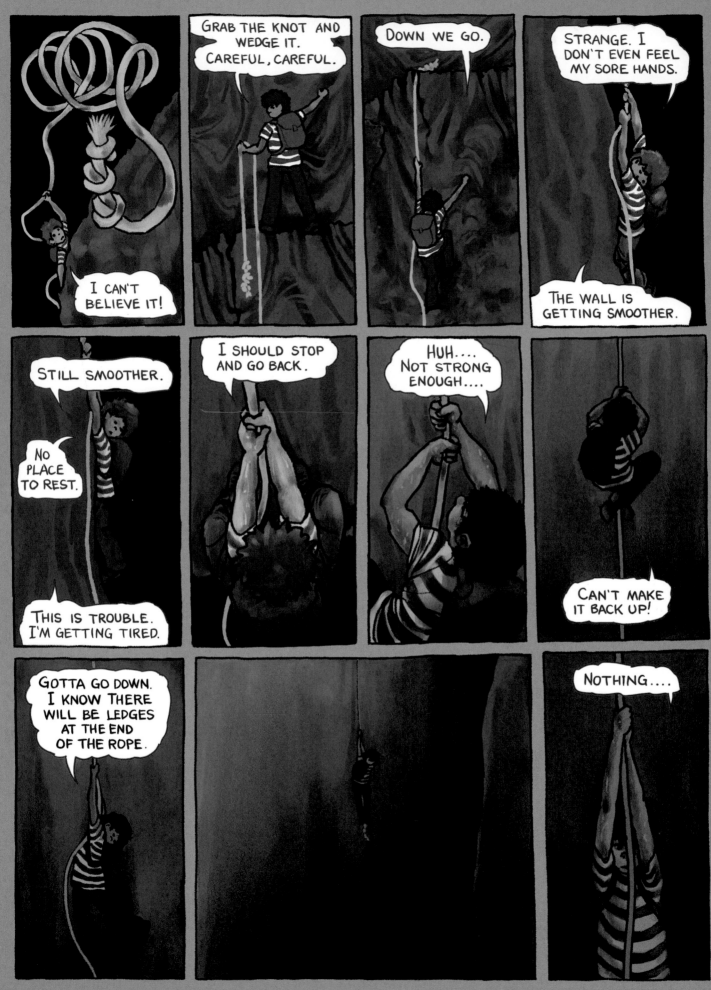

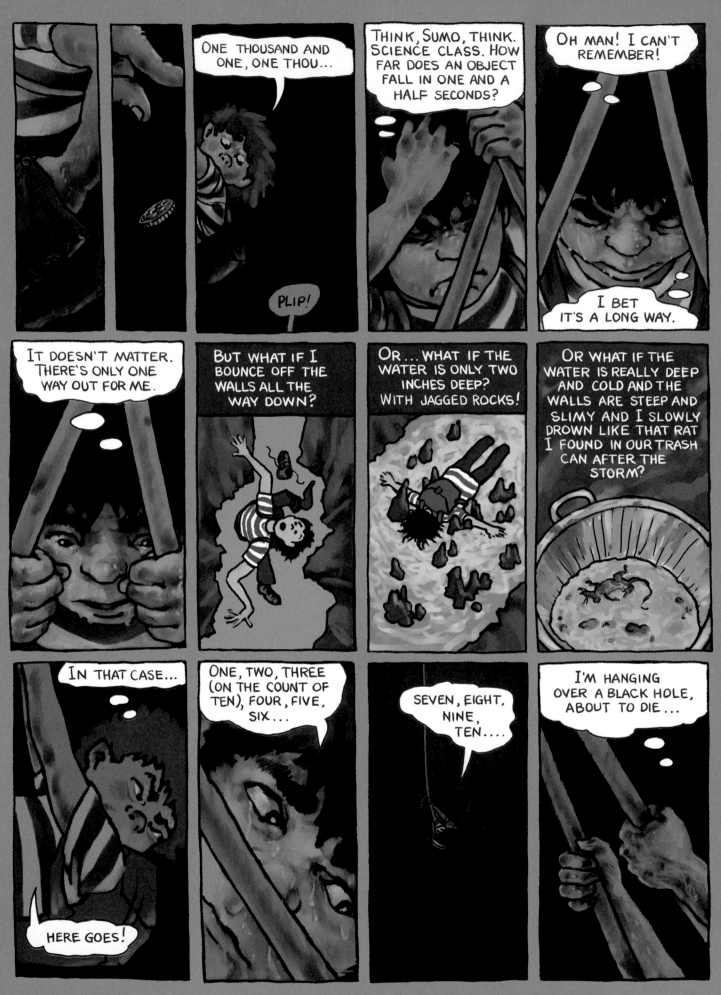

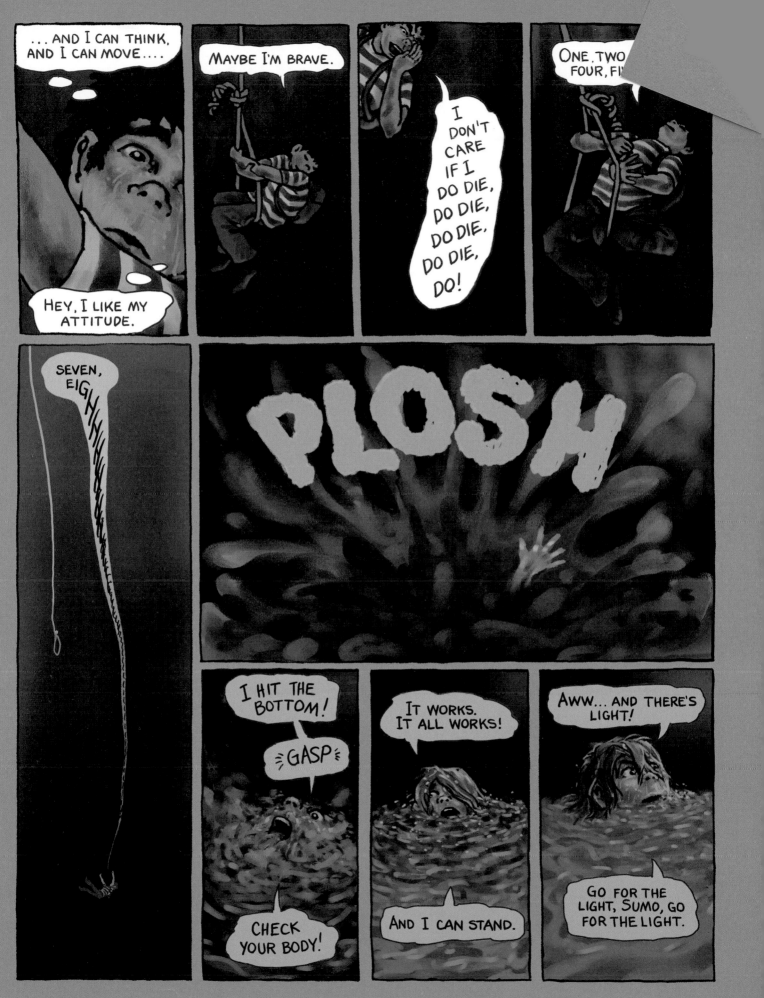

WHMP

It's over now, but the quakes are increasing in frequency and magnitude. This time we were lucky.

We should drop the engines, unload the boat, and use those two oars to paddle out of here.

Wow, Sumo. Your mom doesn't mess around.

I can't leave my engines. I make my living with these.

You get us and our stuff out of here, and I'll buy you new engines.

You know how much these babies cost?

About twelve thousand.

Look.

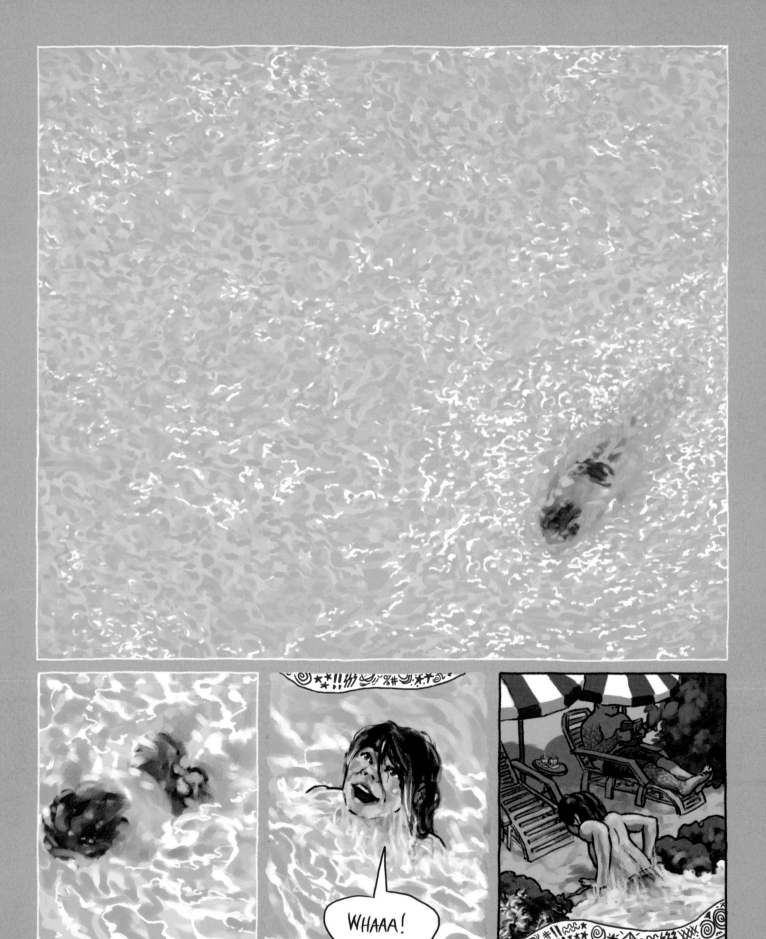

167

WE CAN'T....WE HAVE "BIG MONEY" BACKERS, SUMO... AND ONE THING THAT YOU'LL LEARN IS...

SHHHHHHHHHHH... BIG MONEY LIKES QUIET.

EVEN THE KING IS INVOLVED.

WE'LL BUILD A LAB HERE AND CREATE SO MANY JOBS.

ROADS AND SCHOOLS FOR MY ISLAND... AND I WILL HAVE ENOUGH MATERIAL TO EXPERIMENT WITH FOR THE REST OF MY LIFE! DO YOU KNOW WHAT THAT MEANS?!

IT MEANS WE'LL NEVER GET A CHANCE TO SEE YOU.

OH, SUMO... DON'T SAY THAT. I'VE LEARNED. THIS TIME WE WILL ALL BE PARTNERS, RIGHT FROM THE START.

NOW IT'S YOUR TURN TO TELL ME THE NEWS. I WANT TO KNOW EVERYTHING THAT HAPPENED TO YOU WHILE I WAS GONE. WE'LL "TALK STORY," YEAH?

I AM STILL SO HUNGRY. I MUST HAVE LOST TEN POUNDS.

171

THE END

THIS BOOK IS DEDICATED TO AUDREY WOOD.

THE BLUE SKY PRESS

Copyright © 2008 by Don Wood

All rights reserved.

Library of Congress catalog card number: 2007051084.

ISBN-13 [HC]: 978-0-439-72671-9 / ISBN-10 [HC]: 0-439-72671-9
ISBN-13 [BF]: 978-0-545-10856-0 / ISBN-10 [BF]: 0-545-10856-X

10 9 8 7 6 5 4 3 2 1   08 09 10 11 12
Printed in Singapore   46
First printing, October 2008